Marilyn Lands and Nikki Chenault remind us in their gem of a primer with kind honest words, stories, and beautiful pictures, that grace is all around, waiting for us to notice.

— *Rt. Reverend Glenda S. Curry*
Bishop, Episcopal Diocese of Alabama

This beautifully illustrated book gives helpful, imaginative ideas for anyone who wants to hit a weekly pause button without necessarily observing a full, traditional, 24-hour religious observance, though some will want to try that, too. For beginners who want to create sacred space in their hectic life, A Day of Rest is a practical, on-target balm for our hurried, hurting world.

— *Zara Renander, author of* Labyrinths

A Day of Rest is spiritually power-packed with grace, serenity, beauty, and precious wisdom for living your highest and best life.

— *Rev. Dr. Bayse Holland-Shuey*
Episcopal Priest, Spiritual Director and Educator

A readable and information-packed resource for living, *A Day of Rest* provides an honest and refreshing view of honoring Sabbath as a spiritual practice. Marilyn's and Nikki's work allows for the soul's exploratory relationship with self, others, and God.

— *Jeff Akamatsu, AOJN*
Colonel US Army (Retired) and Spiritual Director

A practical and moving book whose words and pictures invite us into the Divine Life through the pathway of Sabbath keeping. Nikki's photographs capture moments of Sabbath in everyday life and bless us with glimpses into the sacred plan.

— *Rev. Mary Catherine Akamatsu, AOJN*
Executive Director and Co-Founder, Metagem Institute

Nikki Chenault pulls together her many artistic skills in the wondrous culmination of her black and white photography. Her soul continually seeks out the spiritual beauty in life. She captures those moments and holds them up to the light, for all of us to enjoy and meditate upon.

— *Donna Lamb Bowyer*
Commercial Real Estate Investor and World Traveler

Just as a night's sleep is necessary to recharge for the next day, a restful and reflective Sabbath recharges for the next week. This book should be required reading for all, regardless of religious affiliation (or non-affiliation), as a reminder of what the world is about, and the personal balance required to more than endure, but to enjoy the gift of life!

— *Louis B. Weiner, Ph.D.*
President Emeritus, Delta Research, Inc.

DAY OF REST

A Primer on Keeping the Sabbath

DAY OF REST
A Primer on Keeping the Sabbath

ISBN# 978-1-938842-60-3

Interior layout by Bardolf & Company
  www.bardolfandcompany.com

Cover design by Shaw Creative Group

Photo of Nikki Chenault by Ellis Chenault

Author's Dedication

To Walter Brueggemann
who started me on this journey.
And to Abraham Joshua Heschel
who deepened my exploration.
And especially to my husband, Robin
and our son Jordan,
who have been along for the ride.

Photographer's Dedication

To all my spiritual guides who have
enabled me to see my world with new eyes
and capture it through the lens.
And to Lynette, who brings me stability
and wisdom with love.

And from both of us

To our Sabbath Circle friends.
And to the Shekhinah in all of us.

A DAY OF REST

A Primer on
Keeping the Sabbath

by Marilyn Lands

Photographs by Nikki Chenault

Bardolf & Company
Sarasota, Florida

TABLE OF CONTENTS

Author's Preface

I did not grow up in a religious family, but I felt religion calling to me as an adult and, after some searching, I found a church to call home. However, as important as the church community has been for me, nothing has given me peace and serenity like keeping Sabbath. Taking a day of rest spills over into the rest of my week and gives me hope and confidence that all shall be well. Keeping Sabbath has become an essential part of my life. It provides a space to honor the world and discover my role in it—a place of freedom to explore and create. I get to spend time with family and friends, as well as in solitude. I get to slow down and leave the frantic pace of everyday living behind and step into a new rhythm that is more carefree and life affirming. In the process, I recuperate and feel refreshed. Keeping Sabbath has brought grace to how I approach everything. It has changed me, sustained me, and grounded me during challenging times.

I first became aware of this ritual in 2016 in a program conducted by Walter Brueggemann, an influential American Protestant Old Testament scholar and theologian. He was speaking in Birmingham, Alabama, and discussed his book *Sabbath as Resistance: Saying No to the Culture of Now.* It intrigued me enough to read all the Sabbath books I could get my hands on, including Rabbi Abraham Joshua Heschel's classic, *The Sabbath.* Around this time, I traveled to Israel and was able to see firsthand many of the holy sites there. Although I am not Jewish, I was deeply moved by the beauty and history of the land and the customs I experienced.

Along the way, I met people getting ready for Shabbat (Hebrew for "Sabbath"). On Friday afternoon prior to sundown, there was a flurry of activity as they completed last-minute preparations. Then, a quiet descended seemingly out of nowhere, and a sense of peace and reverence replaced the commotion and noise.

I became curious and set out on a quest to learn more about Shabbat. Several people were happy to share their traditions, experiences, and practices. Some invited me to attend their Shabbat service and asked me to stay for dinner. My new friends taught me much, and I began to experiment with keeping my own Sabbath by building on Jewish customs, adding Christian traditions and incorporating rituals that would hold meaning for my family and friends. I also kept reading and discovered Shelly Miller's wonderful book, *Rhythms of Rest*, and her beautiful blog, "Keeping Sabbath." She encouraged readers to start Sabbath circles within their communities, so in 2019 we started a group in North Alabama.

As my practice of keeping Sabbath evolved, I became convinced that sharing my ideas would benefit others as well. I started giving workshops on the topic and wrote articles for journals and magazines. As part of my work as a psychotherapist, I also came to see how this ritual provides much needed self-care in the lives of my clients.

As inspiring as my reading and research was for me, I found that the books didn't help engender enthusiasm in others who expressed an interest. The flood of information felt overwhelming and made the practice appear unrealistic or unattainable. That led to the creation of this primer: a simple little book to share with others the basic concept and ideas for exploring the Sabbath.

Taking a deliberate day of rest each week continues to be an integral part of my existence. The practice has taken a greater hold on my life with each passing year and has impacted me in many wonderful and unexpected ways. I want to share my Sabbath experience with you in these pages and encourage you to do the same: taking a day of rest each week to reorder and reimagine your way of being in the world.

Blessings on your journey!

Marilyn Lands

Photographer's Preface

Incorporating Sabbath keeping into my life is similar to pausing as I look through the lens of my camera. I detach from the busyness of life and exist wholly in the present. Taking a picture happens in a moment. It requires intention to pull away from my daily schedule and set aside a block of time for quiet.

As a child, I had a Kodak Brownie camera. I remember looking through the lens, trying to get the perfect shot. My grandmother, Boo, helped me develop an eye for the visible world. She was an artist and just by being in her presence, I learned that I'm a steward of my world.

As an adult, when I was going through a divorce, I again felt a need for the creative part of me to flourish. I purchased a camera, loaded up on black and white film, and took basic photography classes. Soon I was hooked, and there was no going back!

I believe that black-and-white photography is more dramatic and revealing than color. It brings a clarity of focus, a sharpness and heightened contrast to an image and asks us to pay attention. Because we lead such fast-paced lives, we miss seeing the simple things which make up our world. Taking notice of them and being able to capture them at that moment in time is my goal. I want to convey the sacredness of the here-and-now, always cultivating the unexpected...the passed by... the overlooked.

Each of my images depicts an event in my life. Each photograph is a gift, releasing the intrinsic beauty of the moment. As in my Sabbath practice, being attentive to and mindful of the present, I am able to connect with the event or subject in a way not previously possible.

Nikki Chenault

INTRODUCTION

There are the moments of grace that transcend time, moments of flow, synchronicity or awe. One such moment happened for me while visiting California when I took my son and his friend out for a day to the ocean. We quickly realized that the beach in this area is different from the smooth, white sand dunes of the Gulf Coast. The shore had dark brown sand and was dotted with rocks and stones. Big, fat squirrels played among the boulders. Black flies swarmed all around us. I was not optimistic that our adventure would turn out well. But then I noticed a small wooden cross lodged among the rocks. I picked it up and admired it, wondering about the person who had lost it. It looked like it had once been on a chain, and I held it in my palm like a worry stone.

The boys ran ahead and left me minding our modest beach gear and inadequate hotel towels. I was eager to get back to our rooms when a woman sitting nearby beckoned to me. She was wearing a full-body covering and a hijab. As I approached, she greeted me with a warm smile. She didn't speak English very well but managed to tell me that she had come from Armenia and was visiting the beach with her grandson. While the language barrier made communication difficult, the silence between us felt comfortable. She opened her hamper and shared her picnic, which included grapes that were sweet and juicy. She gave the children cookies and we all gathered on her blanket, enjoying the sunshine. It was a rare moment, one of a very few in my life in which I knew that I was exactly where I was supposed to be.

As we prepared to leave, I gave her the cross I had found. I wanted her to have something to remember the day and our time together. I wasn't sure if the gift was appropriate but felt instinctively that it would be all right. She accepted it with such graciousness that I was overwhelmed with gratitude.

Such moments can happen anywhere, anytime; but we tend to experience them more often during periods of rest and relaxation. When we are busy, we are less likely to notice them. Keeping Sabbath is a wonderful way of allowing time to slow down so we can appreciate grace. By setting our intention to be truly present, we learn to pay attention to what is here and not take for granted the beauty offered up in every moment. In this way, we begin to cultivate a Sabbath heart.

Many people are looking for a way to find more balance in their busy, harried existence. They spend their time working, rushing, striving, making ends meet. Life passes them by as if they were riding in a speeding train or car, their eyes on the road ahead, missing out on the rest. Often, they feel an emptiness inside, a longing for a deeper, greater purpose.

People need a day of rest now more than ever to offset their beleaguered, overburdened lives. We are overwhelmed and overstimulated, yet want instant gratification. We think we thrive on being productive, but it's time to challenge that myth. Taking a day or period of time to rest and reflect allows us to rebalance our lives.

Keeping Sabbath offers an antidote to our stress-filled way of living and can restore us to a more balanced way of being in the world; one that provides time for rest and rejuvenation. It is the best form of self-care on the planet. It is the reset button that allows us to return to our regular life renewed, refreshed, and better able to handle the everyday challenges of the here and now. We have the power to change direction and change the arc of our lives.

The Sabbath gives us opportunity to rest, reflect, and reframe our ideas about work, life and what's truly important. Keeping Sabbath is a way of organizing our days through intentional stopping and mindful pausing to catch up with ourselves and our priorities.

At its most basic, the Sabbath is a day set aside for rest. Historically, it also has been a day of religious observance or prayer. The time has come to reinvent and invigorate this practice to help us examine what rest could look like in modern times.

A metaphor for Sabbath keeping that really resonates with me is the design of a fence. The slats represent the days of the week and the posts that occur at every seventh position remind us that it is our holy time that makes the other days of the week flow smoothly. Ultimately, it is the fence posts that make the fence strong. They provide the structural supports on which the fence is built and can survive. Over time, this regular, consistent time apart will become our architecture in time.

This book is for those who are religious and those who are not, for those who keep Sabbath and for those who have never done so. Whether you believe in God or not is not the point. There are many interpretations about who or what God is or whether there is a God at all. Meister Eckhart, the 13th-century German theologian, philosopher and mystic, reminds us "God is not what you think…or even what you believe, because God is a word unspoken, a thought unthought, a belief unbelieved. So, if you wish to know this God, practice wonder, do what is good and cultivate silence…the rest will follow."

There is no exact plan for taking a day of rest; no right or wrong way of creating this window in time. You will find your way by trial and error, experimenting and discovering what works for you. To that end, this book includes time-honored rituals as well as ideas from many belief systems and traditions, so you can pick and choose what will fit your situation best.

To that end, this book is divided into two parts. The first provides historical perspective and traditions that guide many Sabbath practices and outlines the benefits of taking a day of rest each week. The second explains how keeping Sabbath—including some of the elements of traditional ceremonies—will let you cultivate habits and rituals that are uniquely yours and fit your lifestyle.

Each section of the book is accompanied by beautiful, evocative images. It is our hope that these photographs will invite you to pause, ponder and reflect on the dignity of your own life. You may find them stimulating, illustrative, meditative, or simply enjoyable.

A Day of Rest is our attempt to invite you to join our journey, no matter how or what you believe. There is a Sabbath path for you, and it can change your life for the better. We want to encourage you to embark on your own Sabbath exploration. Along the way, we hope you will discover grace that will allow you to make this practice your own and more deeply experience a new rhythm of life.

Marilyn and Nikki
May 2022

PART ONE

WHY A DAY OF REST

A world without a Sabbath would be like a man without a smile, like a summer without flowers, and like a homestead without a garden. It is the most joyous day of the week.

~ Henry Ward Beecher

Sabbath is God's way of saying "STOP."

~ Adele Ahlberg Calhoun

THE SABBATH
THROUGHOUT HISTORY

*Then God blessed the seventh day and made
it holy because on it he rested from all the work of
creating that he had done.*

— Genesis 2:2-3

A day of rest is not a new idea or even a novel one. It is one of the world's most ancient traditions. In the Jewish faith, the Sabbath (or Shabbat in Hebrew, Shabbos in Yiddish) is considered the holiest of holidays. Keeping Sabbath originated more than 1800 years BCE when, according to Genesis in the Bible, Sarah's lamp, lit on Friday evening, continued to burn throughout the week.

Since then, Jewish people have been keeping the Sabbath, some largely unchanged even in modern times. Jesus, born a Jew, would have kept Sabbath and adhered to the traditions of his time and place. The early Christians continued to keep Sabbath on Saturday but also congregated on Sunday, what they called The Lord's Day, in celebration of Jesus' resurrection. It wasn't until 321 CE when the Emperor Constantine proclaimed Christianity as the official religion of the Roman Empire, that Sunday became established as the weekly day of rest.

Actually, the first mention of the Sabbath in the Bible is the creation story in Genesis where we learn that God was busy for six days making the world but rested on the seventh day. The word Sabbath does not occur in this passage, but "rest" is mentioned three separate times. The Hebrew root word for Shabbat means "to cease" or "to rest," so it seems clear that taking the seventh day to rejuvenate is what God intended for men and women to do.

Many other religious traditions and cultures have some sort of day of rest. Buddhists observe Uposatha every seventh or eighth day, based on the phases of the moon. Many Native American traditions incorporate a day of quiet reflection and prayer on the first day of the new moon. Members of the Bahai Faith take a day of rest on Friday. While Islam does not have a Sabbath ritual, it designates Friday as a day of communal prayer. In many countries, its practitioners observe it with a full or half-day off from work. My Muslim friend Ahmed says that Friday is a special day of prayer.

Many Reform Jews and Christians attend worship services on their holy day, as do those who hold other religious beliefs. Nowadays, non-worshipping Christians typically do not take any sort of day of rest, nor do many secular Jews, although many Reform Jews attend to the Sabbath in some fashion, such as lighting candles after sunset on Fridays. Since the destruction of the temple in 70 CE and second diaspora, many Jewish people have engaged in some form of worship in their homes. For them, religious life has become the heart of their households, a refuge from the world.

Most Americans of a certain age remember blue laws which banned retail sale of liquor and other goods and prohibited certain activities, like dancing and theater performances on Sundays for religious reasons. They got their name from the blue paper on which the early Puritan settlers of American printed the Sunday restrictions. Although blue laws have become less common in our more secular times, they are still enforced in parts of the

United States and Canada, and in European countries like Poland, where most stores must remain closed on Sundays.

Still, the trend world-wide has been toward eliminating any religion-based restrictions to commerce and cultural events on Saturdays and Sundays. This may be due to a number of factors, including an increase in populations that no longer have any religious affiliation and the demands of capitalist economies to provide access to free markets at all times.

Whatever the case, this development has come with a heavy price. We are overworked and weary. Technology has blurred the boundaries between work and home, and there is constant pressure to get everything done now. We are constantly checking our communication devices and worried that we're missing out on something. Religion is no longer the anchor of our lives, and people are leaving various church denominations today in record numbers.

Yet, people are still searching for a deeper, more spiritual meaning and purpose for their existence. And, we all need rest, no matter what we believe or what our spiritual life looks like. Perhaps that is why the concept of keeping Sabbath is resonating with so many people today.

SABBATH BENEFITS

Sabbath is about rest and laying down our burdens.
It is a vacation from the demands of the week
and an introduction to shift gears and slow down.

— Mirabai Starr

Many people pay lip service to creating work/life balance but err on the side of too much work and too little life. Taking a day of rest is an antidote to our current frenzied way of living. Keeping Sabbath gives us the opportunity to reflect and restore this balance directly. We can do this by deliberately setting time apart, intentional focus and paying attention to how we spend our days.

In my role as a psychotherapist, I often tell my clients that there are three simple things that, if practiced, would alleviate many mental health issues.

1. More silence
2. More time spent outdoors
3. More physical activity

In our modern world, we are no longer comfortable with silence. Many clients tell me that they keep the radio or TV on, not to listen or watch, but simply to have some background noise because they can't bear the quiet. And yet, silence can be soothing and act as an antidote to our noise-filled world.

Part of your Shabbat experience should include stillness and silence. Turning inward allows us to sense the movement in tranquility and the sound of an orchestra that plays in the peace we have created. The gentler rhythms of a day of rest provide opportunities for contemplation and pleasurable pursuits.

Recent research about happiness has shown that time spent outdoors is crucial to our wellbeing and can translate to the rest of our days. If we can combine being outside with physical activity, we can reap double benefits. Walking in city parks or hiking in the countryside are excellent Sabbath pursuits, as are bicycling and gardening. I like to wander around my yard and pick a bouquet of flowers and herbs to make a lovely arrangement for our Sabbath table. That may not qualify for dual benefits, but it adds to my enjoyment and provides a visual feast.

Other advantages of taking a day of rest include attaining simplicity, mindfulness, and a greater sense of equilibrium.

Cultivating simplicity allows us to move away from constant multitasking and choose to do just one thing at a time instead. Studies show that we are more attentive when focusing on a single activity because we are fully present and not distracted by trying to do several things at once.

Along the way, we can return to a sense of childlike wonder. I remember one Sunday at the beach when our son was very young. As we were collecting shells, I was looking for the perfect and the pristine while my son kept putting cracked shells into our basket. I gently explained that those were broken and should be tossed back into the ocean. "But Mommy, they're beautiful," he said. When I looked at them again—really looked—I had to admit that he was right. Their rugged edges had a presence of their own. He hadn't picked them at random but found shells whose shapes were pleasing to the eye. Many of them are still on display in our home. My son taught me an important lesson that day, including that we can learn a great deal from children and from others, if we take the time to pay attention.

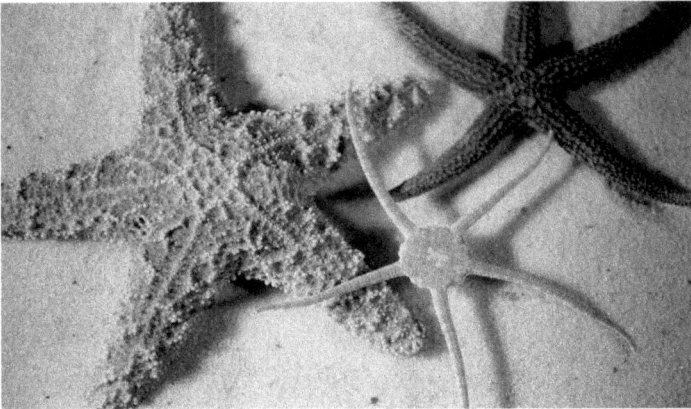

Along my Sabbath journey, I had the privilege of meeting Shelly Miller, author of *Rhythms of Rest,* for tea in the Victoria and Albert Museum in London and hear more about her Sabbath practices. She began her day-of-rest process to counter the loneliness she felt after moving far away from home. Nowadays, more people than ever suffer from isolation and loneliness. Keeping Sabbath always gives us something to look forward to. We have the option of meeting others in person or via video conferencing technologies, or of spending time alone.

Sabbath keeping can also bring unexamined aspects of our lives into sharp focus. For me, this led to the realization of how much of the stuff I had amassed cluttered up my life. I longed for a more organized home that I could truly enjoy. Coincidentally, I had heard about a 30-day challenge for decluttering. On day one of the month, you get rid of one thing, on day two, two things and so on. On the last day, you are up to eliminating a daunting 30 things. I decided to try it. The challenge was both difficult and exhilarating. I got rid of many decorative items that we had collected over the years and no longer appreciated. That resulted in being able to truly see the things I chose to keep. The hardest thing was parting with some of my books, but I've learned to use a Kindle for novels and to check out audio books from our local library. Since completing the challenge, I feel my home is more enjoyable and easier to clean. It has become a truly comfortable space for my family and me. I would not have made it so if I hadn't "discovered" decluttering during one of my days of rest.

A day of rest can act as a rejuvenating force. We can achieve this by taking pauses, going more slowly, and leaving room to breathe around the activities of the day to relish them fully. We can move at a different pace, strip away the superficial, and examine the priorities in our lives as well as what gets in our way. We can take our time and savor each moment.

We can spend time with friends and family or engage in solitary pursuits. We can rediscover things that make us passionate. The more we take time to rest and the more balanced our lives become, the more energy and zest we'll have for the rest of the week.

OTHER ASPECTS
OF KEEPING SABBATH

One obstacle I hear frequently about keeping Sabbath is that people simply do not have the time to take a day of rest. For myself, I find the opposite to be true. Preserving this time apart allows me to return to my regular life rested and refreshed, giving me clarity and perspective. After a day of rest, I feel renewed and eager to greet Monday morning with anticipation and vigor.

In this section we will discuss some additional aspects of Sabbath keeping, including how to practice it while on the road, as well as the feminine characteristics of the day and social justice engagement.

TRAVELING

Traveling God presents the Sabbath rest
as a shelter we enter.

— Charles Swindoll

When traveling away from home for business or pleasure, it is possible to keep Sabbath by focusing on essential aspects of the rituals. Depending on your plans, you may be able to incorporate most of your typical practices and perhaps even add a few that honor your destination. Whether alone in a hotel or with family and friends, you can take time to say blessings for your near and dear ones. You may have only a few minutes or half an hour to set aside for meditation and affirmations but you'll find it's worth it as a way to keep your practice moving forward and feeling alive.

Take the opportunity to be creative and examine your priorities. Think about the essentials that you could pack for continuing your practice while away and create your own Sabbath travel kit. It is even possible to order such a kit designed for this purpose online.

I use a beautiful, embroidered bag in which I carry a small candle, matches, a silver plate for holding the candle, and a prayer book designed for travelers. I also bring a lovely small bird decoration and put it on the desk or dresser to remind me that I'm in a special time. Taking along a talisman from home, a small framed photo of a loved one, or a family picture, or a book of poetry can all enhance the experience. I also pick up wine when I reach my destination to help me celebrate the Sabbath. The possibilities are endless, so long as they provide meaning for you.

Traveling can also provide opportunities to experience how others celebrate the Sabbath. During one of our trips to Israel, in the city of Jaffa, I happened to strike up a conversation with the owner of a shop about Shabbat, and she invited my husband and me to her synagogue's service that Friday. Excited, Rob and I wandered to the address she had given me to find the door locked and no one else around. We decided to wait in the nearby courtyard and little by little others started to join us. Finally, when the door to the temple opened, we all made our way inside—men to the left, women to the right, and a curtain in between—and grabbed a book for the service. It was in Hebrew. Fortunately, one of the people we'd talked to in the courtyard made sure we both had the English version of the book in our hands.

Once all were settled the service began. I enjoyed the readings, chants, and songs very much. Later, Rob told me that, throughout the service, one of the men sitting next to him did his best to point out where they were in his English book. The most memorable part of the evening for him happened toward the end of the service during one of the more uplifting songs. Suddenly, most of the men got up from their benches and danced in a perfect conga line on their side of the temple. Rob said they jumped up and down with such joy that, had there been lampshades in the room, they would have plopped them on their heads as they danced around! This unexpected experience was a gift demonstrating that, although Shabbat is considered a time of quiet and introspection, it can have moments of great exuberance and celebration.

CELEBRATING THE FEMININE

It is the woman who ushers in the joy
and sets up the most exquisite symbol, light to
dominate the atmosphere of the home.

— Abraham Joshua Heschel

Most religions refer to God in non-inclusive masculine language. This allows little room for the feminine to have a role in religious services. In many traditions, women are not allowed to serve as ministers, priests, rabbis, or even Sunday school teachers. This creates an arbitrary duality that denies younger generations female role models or mentors. Yet earlier traditions believed that Wisdom (sometimes known as Sophia) was female and the Psalms of the Old Testament pay tribute to her.

Historically, the female in the household played an essential role in the Sabbath celebration and not just by cooking and cleaning. She recited the prayers over the candles and her partner recited prayers of praise to her.

In some Jewish traditions, the Sabbath is also known as Shekhinah. The feminine Hebrew word, meaning "dwelling" or "settling," refers to the divine presence of God. It does not occur in the Bible but comes from rabbinical and mystical literature. The Kaballah, a set of esoteric interpretations within Judaism, associates the Shekinah with the female attributes of God.

Some Kabbalist teachings even consider the Sabbath an actual person—a bride or queen, who should be invited at the beginning of the Sabbath's opening ritual on Friday evening to welcome the divine feminine into one's home. It is as if we are anticipating a special guest and need to make proper arrangements to establish an atmosphere of hospitality. The tradition of the Shekhinah as the Sabbath bride continues to this day.

Another belief regarding the Shekhinah is that we are given a second soul on Shabbat that remains with us during that time each week and then departs. According to author Mirabai Starr, a leading voice in the interspiritual movement, Shekhinah is an indwelling presence that resides in exile during the week but comes home again on Shabbat.

It isn't necessary to get into the nitty-gritty of these ideas while celebrating your day of rest. We live in a time of increasing diversity, however, when traditional gender roles are being questioned and redefined. So, as you develop your Sabbath practice, you may want to pay attention to the balance of masculine and feminine energies. You may find it a rich area to explore, mine, and utilize to enhance your day of rest and tailor it to your own needs.

ENCOURAGING SOCIAL ENGAGEMENT

Sabbath is both a contemplative practice and an act of social and environmental justice.

— Mirabai Starr

For some, engaging in contemplation on the Sabbath leads them to recognize the world's ills and problems and to address them in tangible ways.

In the Jewish tradition, charitable giving—tzedakah—is considered a moral obligation. One common form historically was to set aside a portion of the harvest to distribute to the poor. In time it evolved, and for many families it is the first act of the Sabbath, an act of compassion, however small, to help relieve suffering. A special tzedakah box or container is set out and each member of the family, and even guests contribute whatever they can. Children can join in, too, by contributing their dollars or quarters. Participants can decide together on the organization that will receive these special funds.

Some people use their solitary Sabbath time to read books or articles about social justice and issues that concern us. The knowledge gathered can be translated into action and advocacy during the rest of the week.

We can also be more mindful of our care for this planet and refrain from excessive shopping and consuming. We can offer acts of service and kindness. One friend I know makes it a Sabbath practice to write encouraging notes to friends and acquaintances who have touched her life, as a way of planting seeds of hope.

If you have chosen to not go anywhere on this day, you can commit to volunteering for a worthy organization or an activity during the upcoming week, such as buying coats for the homeless. By not driving your vehicle for one day, we reduce our carbon footprint.

Think creatively about how small acts can make a difference. One small step my family takes is the way we eat. We try to only purchase sustainable seafood for our seventh-day meal. For our Sabbath breakfast, we save our leftover rice and whatever vegetables might be starting to "show their age" and turn them into a colorful and crispy treat topped with cheese.

The Sabbath gives us a very real opportunity to reprioritize our lives, focus on what really matters, and connect with our Creator, Mother Earth, our God, or our higher power, as well as with ourselves and our families.

PART TWO

CREATING YOUR OWN
DAY OF REST

*Anybody can observe Sabbath, but making it
holy surely takes the rest of the week.*

— Alice Walker

BACKGROUND

Imagine having a sacrament named thanks!
~ Walter Brueggemann

Sabbath in the Jewish tradition typically begins at sunset on Friday evening and ends one hour after sunset on Saturday, adding up to 25 hours of time that is set apart. I find this bonus hour a part of the wonder and magic of this special day. Sabbath can allow us to empty ourselves of the myriad things occupying our mind each week and make room for God or other matters of importance.

There is no proper or correct way to practice keeping the Sabbath. There is only the process of finding what makes time sacred or special for you. We can follow the customs of our chosen religion, pick and choose from several belief systems, or develop our own personalized plan. We can make this time apart as religious, secular or artistic as we please. And, no matter what we do, we can be confident that it is all good.

The Bible offers little in the way of instruction except that we cease from work, rest and remember. The point is you get to decide. What do you define as work, stressful activities and draining drudgery? What brings you joy, pleasure and relaxation? Spend some time making a list for each category. Then put the list in a Sabbath basket to use during your day of rest when appropriate.

Because of my visits to Israel, I started with Jewish practices I had observed and experienced, using them as a template. I incorporated Christian customs and prayers, primarily from the

Episcopal Book of Common Prayer. Over time I began writing my own prayers and added aspects from other traditions that interested me, such as Zen Buddhism, until the ceremony felt truly unique and matched my belief system. It now includes elements that create a feast for all the senses: seeing, smelling, tasting, touching and hearing.

As you develop your practice, you can do likewise, and it might stay the same throughout your journey, or may change, as mine did. The ideas presented here are not intended to be prescriptive but rather to give the reader a basic framework at the start. I hope it provides inspiration and that you will tailor your practice with meaningful rituals that speak to you.

Just as how we define work varies for each of us, so does how we define rest and what we choose to remember. Your Sabbath practice will evolve over time, so take time to plan and ponder. Embrace the journey.

STARTING YOUR PRACTICE

*A life built upon Sabbath is contented because
in the rhythms of rest we discover
our time is full of the holiness of God.*

— Shelly Miller

If you are a novice at Sabbath keeping, it may be helpful to start gradually. Trying to do too much in the beginning can get overwhelming, and you may feel like tossing in the towel before experiencing all the joy and wonder of taking a day of rest.

There are four activities and times that are most evocative of observing the Sabbath:

- Preparation
- The first evening's prayers and meal
- The next morning, which often includes worship
- The Sabbath afternoon

You don't have to do any or all of these. However, many seasoned practitioners suggest beginning with the evening service. You can take a simplified approach as you begin setting this time apart. Light a candle and recite a few blessings. Open and drink the wine. Share the bread or whatever food you've chosen for the occasion and enjoy the evening meal with family and friends, or by yourself as a solitary pursuit.

A mother and daughter I met while traveling told me that the Sabbath is the best thing, even if you are not religious. They love lighting the candles, raising the cup of wine and giving thanks.

Once you have established a basic practice, gradually add other activities that appeal to you. Be creative and enjoy the process. Review the checklist in the appendix that details potential activities to add into your day of rest, as well as possible items to reduce or eliminate during this time. Decide on a few from each category to begin incorporating into your practice. Your approach may be very different from mine, but that is what will make it meaningful for you. Again, it's easier to start small and make changes and additions to your new routine as it begins to take shape.

I suggest that you make your Sabbath distinctly different from your ordinary time. If you are in the habit of taking a daily walk, consider going on a meditative excursion or a hike instead. It can be as short as around the block. Or go rowing, kayaking or canoeing on a lake or river.

If you cook most days of the week, you might want to order a take-out meal or opt for delivery. If you don't read much, you might enjoy an inspirational poem or short story. If you read a lot, consider choosing something different from your typical fare; perhaps a special devotional book reserved for the Sabbath.

PREPARATION

Sabbath requires careful planning, repeated planting, and constant protection.

— Alicia Britt Chloe

If you are like most of us, the boundary between your work and personal time has probably become quite blurred. Think intentionally about how you want your Sabbath to unfold and plan accordingly. As you go about the business of your week, be thinking about what preparations need to be made: who to invite, what groceries to buy, what you will need to have on hand or prepare ahead of time? Perhaps you'll iron the tablecloth or pick up bread, chocolates and/or flowers.

Think about when, where, what and how to organize your day of rest. Remember that you'll want to embark on a shift from head space to heart space. Visualize the details. What suggests rest to you? Decide when you will have your Sabbath celebration and how much time you want to take in the beginning. If you can't commit to a weekly observance at first, try bi-weekly or monthly. If being at home is too much of a distraction, consider signing up for an organized retreat or booking your own time at a sanctuary location that speaks to your soul. The goal is to nurture your soul, and you alone know what that requires of you. The Appendix contains a list of resources, including books and websites, if you are looking for more information or ideas.

Make a list and look at your calendar to pencil in tasks so you will know when you can make time for them. You may want to clean your house the afternoon before the Sabbath or right before your chosen time to celebrate. Take a bath or shower and dress in clean clothes that allow you to feel special.

In preparing for the Sabbath, consider organizing the tools you will need to make everything happen effectively. In our house, we set a fine linen placemat on the counter with a candle, matches, a plate for bread or crackers, along with a cover for them, and our tzedakah box so that we are ready when dusk comes.

Following are a few items that I find helpful for organizing my Sabbath space and time. They include a container for storing items that I don't want to intrude on this special time, a basket to hold objects reserved for Sabbath time, and a notebook or notepad for jotting down things to remember after the day of rest is over.

Box for Everyday Things

It's good to have a special box, small cabinet, or empty drawer in which to deposit items you don't want to use during your day of rest:

- Car keys
- Cell phone
- TV remote
- Computer mouse
- Apple watch
- Wallet
- Check book
- Other items that can represent an item too large to fit in your box or drawer

I include my phone and car keys. I shut down my laptop and close my computer screen. My purse, with my wallet and checkbook, remains in the closet. I don't watch television during my day of rest and refrain from shopping or driving anywhere.

You will need to create your own list based on typical distractions. This is your Sabbath, so your box or drawer may look different, and that's okay. You might also put an item in the box during the week—a cross, icon, or other meaningful object—and bring it out for your day of rest to remind you of its special quality. I have a small decorative bird that I put on my kitchen counter, and it remains there during the Sabbath as a visual reminder that this time is different. Looking at it never ceases to make me smile.

BASKET

Consider designating a basket to keep your special prayer or poetry books for Sabbath reading, as well as other items gathered throughout the week that you want to save for the more leisurely hours on your day of rest. Perhaps include some art supplies and a sketch book. Whenever you don't have time for an article you want to read or a letter that needs more thought and time to ponder, drop it in the basket. When the Sabbath arrives you will have it handy for uninterrupted exploration.

I always have at least one fiction and one nonfiction book in my basket because I know there will be ample time for reading. Because I love to indulge in good self-care practices on my day of rest, I also keep some luxurious hand cream and a facial mask in my basket for my nap time.

Other items might include a special pair of socks or slippers for feeling cozy and relaxed. You might designate a beautiful journal and pen to be used only during this distinctive time.

NOTEBOOK

Another tool that helps organize your Sabbath is a notebook and pen (in your basket) for jotting down anything that needs to be recorded and transferred later to your weekly calendar, grocery list, etc. That way you don't have to go to your calendar or mobile device, which breaches the Sabbath boundaries and can lead you down a rabbit hole of distractions. Putting these items into the book and out of your mind allows you to focus on the special activities instead.

When the day of rest is over, do any tasks that are simple and can be accomplished easily, and write the others on a to-do list. I also like to keep a log of Sabbath start times in the front of my notebook. This gives me a real sense of how the year, seasons and daylight change.

Depending on where you live, winter Sabbaths differ in many respects from those in the spring, summer or fall if you adhere to the sunset rule. Keeping a log is one simple way to remember the rhythm of our days, the seasons and our connection to the solar system and universe beyond.

In summary, preparations help you anticipate the special time of your day of rest and create the right frame of mind and space for holy celebration. Use the checklist in the Appendix to help determine your preparatory steps and check them off as completed. Good preparation will help you make the transition from the ordinary week to your unique day of rest feel seamless and achievable.

OPENING THE DAY OF REST

In the beginner's mind there are many possibilities,
but in the expert's there are few.

— Shunryu Suzuki

For this section, I have chosen to use the elements of the Jewish Sabbath, as I understand them, as a starting point. They have the longest history and can provide a template for developing your own practices, including candle lighting, wine, hand washing, bread, meals, and worship. This list isn't intended to be exclusive or limiting, so you should feel free to add or subtract to it as suits your lifestyle. To that end, I have included suggestions and alternatives for varying the practices. Do not hesitate to modify or build on them to fit your experience.

Traditionally, Shabbat starts at sundown on Friday, but you can choose whatever time works best for you. For Jewish practitioners, the ritual begins with candle lighting, blessings, prayer, and sharing of bread. Some families also include the washing of hands. Feel free to add prayers from your own tradition, write your own prayers, recite poetry, or simply speak from the heart.

While it is customary to spend Sabbath time with family, inviting friends is also encouraged. Experiencing a day of rest is a celebration, after all, and sharing it with others is a special gift. In many Jewish traditions there is a blessing for each spouse and each child. You might want to include a blessing or gratitude for each additional family member and guest present. Perhaps light a candle for each participant or have just one for the entire group.

Because my husband and I do considerable socializing during the week, we usually keep Sabbath without guests, unless our son is visiting. He participates in all the Sabbath rituals with us and often chooses the recipient of the week's tzedekah funds. When we do invite guests, it is for our Saturday night meal. We try to limit our conversation to happy topics and generally avoid discussions of recent news, personal tragedies, and politics.

Don't forget to include your pets—cats, dogs, birds, turtles and others—on the Sabbath. They are, after all, part of your family, and you can spend time playing with them and giving them a special treat. The people and animals gathered are all blessings in our lives and you honor them with your acknowledgment.

OPENING STATEMENT

As you start your day of rest, you enter a special space and time, and you might want to mark crossing that threshold with a prayer, poem, blessing or opening statement. Pick something that is meaningful to your practice and that signifies that something significant is about to begin.

Below is a statement I wrote to honor this time. Feel free to use it, adapt it, or come up with something of your own.

*We gather for this Sabbath to offer thanks
for the many gifts and joys of this life.*

*May we receive them gratefully, tend them
graciously, and share them generously.*

*We seek rest, refreshment, and restoration
for ourselves, our friends and family, and
all those who share our earthly home.*

*We strive to cultivate contemplation so that we
may be receptive to the word of truth. May this
truth move us to serve others with compassion.*

*We pray that eyes will be opened to the beauty
of creation, hearts to the dignity of mankind,
and minds to the mystery beyond us.*

*May this sacred time allow us to dwell in the
present moment and to grow in wisdom
and grace, so that we might be a blessing
in the week to come.*

Amen

CANDLE LIGHTING

There are two ways of spreading light:
to be the candle or the mirror that reflects it.

~ Edith Wharton

The Friday night candle lighting ceremony dates to the first century and has become the tradition most associated with the Jewish Shabbat. It signifies the end of the week and begins the Sabbath celebration. Lighting a candle can evoke the sense of reverence in all of us, no matter what we believe.

Candle lighting generally coincides with sunset in the Jewish ritual but can begin as early as 18 minutes before to provide some wiggle room for preparations to be completed. If you miss the actual time of sunset, you can still keep Sabbath, but without lighting candles. Of course, you can make your own rules here, too, and set your own schedule.

The candles are often placed on a decorative metal or mirrored tray and should be visible from the table where the meal will take place. It is customary to employ a match rather than a lighter and not to extinguish the used match but to place it on the metal tray and let it burn down on its own. Candle lighting is certainly central to the celebration of the Sabbath and brings beauty to our homes. It reminds us of the sacred in our lives.

For Jewish practitioners, the Sabbath has an emphasis on the feminine and the woman head of household has a specific role to play. One of these is lighting the candles on Friday night. However, candles should be lit even if no woman is present, and it might feel more appropriate to rotate this role among all members in a family or offer the privilege to your guests. Once the candles are lit, a woman brings the smoke forward with her hands three times and then covers her eyes as she recites the blessing. Most households use two or more candles. Couples often receive a set as a wedding gift and some families add a new candlestick for each child. In our household of three people, we opt for using a large candle with three wicks.

The candlesticks along with other ceremonial items, including the Kiddush cup and plate, and tzedakah box, are often prized possessions that remain on display throughout the week in a prominent spot in the house, such as a side table, mantle, or glass cabinet. This serves to remind us of the holiness of the home and that we all can act in the role of officiating the Sabbath ceremony.

Here are some alternatives to lighting candles as the opening ceremony to your day of rest.

- Burning incense
- Having a fire in the fireplace or outdoors
- Listening to a favorite piece of music
- Setting up a temporary altar
- Engaging in a session of breathwork
- Meditating
- Doing Yoga or Tai Chi
- Chanting
- Invoking a sacred word or mantra and then repeating it during your Sabbath time
- Journaling
- Saying a prayer

WINE

Wine and friends are a great blend.
— Ernest Hemingway

The wine, traditionally red, is served in a special Kiddush cup with a petal-shaped handle and base. In Hebrew the word "kiddush" means "sanctification," and the blessing or benediction recited over the cup signifies that this wine is not simply for drinking but something of greater meaning. Mirabai Starr writes in her book, *Wild Mercy: Living in the Fierce and Tender Wisdom of the Women Mystics*, "The empty cup is a symbol of the heart that cries out in longing for God."

The cup may be shared by all participants, or each may have their own individual cup or glass. At our house we use two lovely pottery vessels that we bought at a local art festival. During the sanctification, it is possible to substitute poetry or music for prayers and blessings. Another option is to have a basket in which prayer requests on slips of paper are deposited throughout the week to be read during this time.

Alternatives to wine:
- Grape juice
- Sparkling water
- A carafe of water infused with fresh fruit slices
- Champagne
- Iced tea mixed with lemonade
- Hot tea or mulled wine
- A Sabbath cocktail
- A special drink for the children such as cocoa or chocolate milk

HAND WASHING

Water flows over these hands
May I use them skillfully
As I construct and shape this day.

— Thich Nhat Hanh

Many Jewish Sabbath practitioners wash their hands before the breaking of the bread. Some historians have dated this ritual all the way back to the purification practices of the priests in the first temple that King Solomon built around 1000 BCE. For people who performed manual labor, the cleaning of hands serves both for purposes of hygiene and spiritual purification.

Over a large water bowl, pass a filled cup to your left hand and pour water three times over the right hand. Then do the same for the other hand. As you dry your hands, you may want to recite an appropriate blessing. The traditional Jewish blessing is: *Blessed are you Lord, our God, King of the universe, who has instructed us with His commandments and commanded us regarding the washing of the hands.*

If you like, you can use the special two-handled cup that is often part of the Jewish hand washing ritual. This ensures that you don't become contaminated by your yet-to-be-cleaned hand as you transfer the cup from one hand to the other.

The act of washing one's hands can play an important symbolic role in the process of transitioning from the regular week to the Sabbath's special time of rest and renewal. It can also provide a physical act to reaffirm the mental thought process involved in setting the past week aside and, as if to wash one's hands of it—literally and figuratively—to focus the day of rest on ourselves, our families, and our relationship with God.

BREAD

There is not a thing more positive than bread.
— Feyodor Dostoyevsky

Bread is often symbolic of all food and represents reverence for the Earth, its bounty and the harvest. The breaking of bread as an invitation to one's home, an act of friendship and sharing, is a custom in many cultures. Jews traditionally use challah, a braided bread brushed with an egg white. Challah is often served with salt to enhance the flavor and as a reminder of man's eternal covenant with God because salt never spoils. Frequently two loaves are served to represent the double portion of manna the Israelites received during the 40 years in the wilderness following their exodus from Egypt.

The bread is set upon the table and topped with a decorative cover. After the blessing, the bread is then shared, with participants each tearing off a piece and enjoying the flavor and bounty. In my home we use a gluten free cracker. It's amazing how delicious it is all on its own and a delight to savor on the tongue. You might try a bread from your homeland such as focaccia, baguette, or sourdough, or an entirely different type of food you consider a treat. You can cover it with a family heirloom napkin or a decorative piece of fabric. Having a distinctive plate that is used every week helps to instill the sense of continuity and that what is happening is special.

Suggested Alternative Practices:

- Baking your own bread
- Using bread with dipping sauce
- Sharing gratitude
- Saying a prayer or blessing for farmers
- Eating a piece of chocolate
- Serving cookies or cake
- Sharing fruit

MEALS

*Food may be essential as fuel for the body
but good food is fuel for the soul.*

~ Malcolm Forbes

There are several opportunities for formal meals during the day of rest period, notably on the evening before, and breakfast and lunch the next day. Meal preparation can be simple or elaborate, whichever corresponds to your idea of Sabbath keeping and works for your family.

Susanah Heschel describes that, growing up, meals in her home were always the same: challah from the local bakery, chicken soup, Cornish game hens, salad and vegetables. For dessert, her father peeled an apple, keeping the pared skin in one long, unbroken string. The mother and daughter I mentioned earlier in starting your practice have a simple meal of chicken soup every Friday night. In the Jewish tradition, once Sabbath begins no work can be done. That includes using the on-and-off knobs on stoves, ovens and microwaves. When I visited Tel Aviv, I found that some Israeli families enjoy a leisurely Sabbath by staying at a hotel. Everything needed is provided, the meals are kosher, and traditional worship is available on the premises. The afternoons are often spent lounging on the beautiful beaches there.

In our home, we usually eat seafood for our Saturday evening meal, prepare a simple breakfast of crunchy rice with bits of our leftover vegetables. We have a lunch tray of cheeses, olives, vegetables, and sardines. That may not be everyone's first choice, but it works for us. It's simple to prepare—a feast for the eyes as well as the stomach.

The times when you eat meals and the food choices you make and can vary with the time of year and daylight.

Some ideas for meals:

- A rotisserie chicken with a loaf of bread, cheese and grapes
- A charcuterie board
- Your favorite delivered pizza
- Take-out Chinese food
- Chicken soup

- Fish or seafood
- A vegetarian dish
- Make ahead dishes like casseroles, soup or stew
- Breakfast for dinner
- Trying new recipes
- Going out to your favorite restaurant

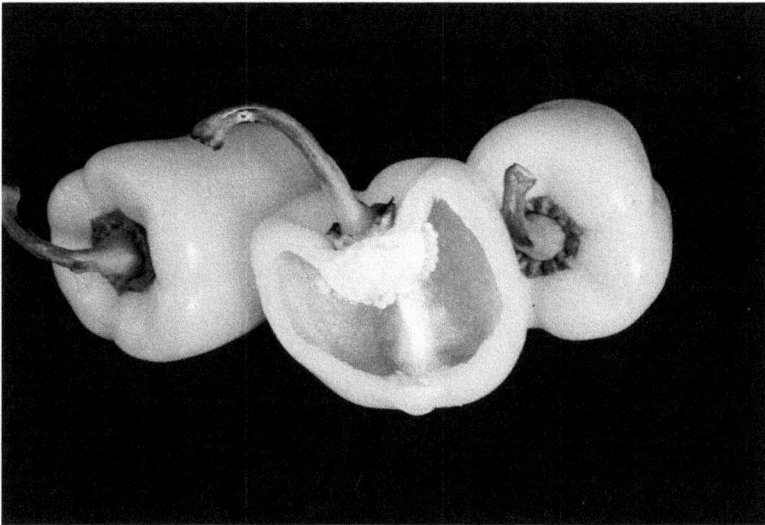

Ultimately, how you choose to handle meals during the Sabbath should support your priorities for this special day. If your week was hectic, you might want to prepare a nice meal in a leisurely fashion to slow down, unwind, and focus on your family. On the other hand, if cooking meals contributes to what makes your week feel chaotic, then picking up something simple from the grocery store or going out to eat may be just the treat you need to help clear your mind and relax your body.

How you eat your meals can also contribute to your Sabbath experience. In our house during the week, my husband

and I often have our evening meal in front of the TV—both of our families did the same as we grew up. On our day of rest, we try to break that pattern. We take the Sabbath candle and dinner plates into the dining room and conduct our conversations and appreciation of the meal before us accordingly. Again, choose what works best for you—how about an indoor picnic!—to separate this special time from the regular week and help bring a sense of calm and peace to you and your family.

WORSHIP

For many people, Sabbath is a day to attend services at a church, temple or synagogue, but worshiping in a public place is not required. Many parts of religious ceremonies can be performed perfectly well at home. This lets us worship in whatever way we desire no matter where we are and allows us to take a greater role in the creation of meaningful ritual. During the Coronavirus pandemic lockdown in 2020, I found keeping Sabbath was a way to stay true to my beliefs despite being separated from my community.

Your worship practice might look very different from the traditional religious service. Perhaps a symphony concert or visit to an art museum will feel more like appropriate devotion to you. A nature hike or visit to the botanical garden could be the perfect meditative ritual. The poet and novelist Wendell Berry, in his book of Sabbath poems, admits that he is "a bad-weather church goer" and that on most days he "is drawn to the woods on the local hillsides or along the streams." He shares that some days poems come and some days they don't. Nevertheless, both kind of days are Sabbath days.

Prayer and worship do not have to be based in words or scripture. Words rarely manage to fully express our deepest feelings. Some of the richest prayer life happens with multi-sensory practices.

The whirling dervishes of the Sufi tradition practice a form of physically active meditation by twirling rapidly with arms open and the right hand directed toward the sky to receive God's gifts to them. Yoga, an ancient Indian tradition, is meant to cleanse one's body and mind and has meditative aspects. The Romantic poets and composers sought the divine in nature, and we can too.

One visual prayer practice is Visio Divina, or Divine Seeing—the process of meditating and praying while looking at an image: a work of art, a stained glass window, a garden, a religious icon, or a photograph. In religious traditions it is a special way of inviting God to speak to one's heart. But it can be used as a contemplative form of self-discovery as well. Nikki's practice of Visio Divina has helped her view all aspects of her life through a sacred lens, which has enriched her day-to-day experience manifold.

Visio Divina can be done with any of the images in this book. Here's how:

- Pick a comfortable place where you will not be disturbed. Identify a photo for reflection. Close your eyes, relax, breathe deeply, and center yourself.

- Look at the photo and meditate on the image as whole, then identify any part that especially captivates you.

- Ask yourself why you are drawn to it. Does meditating on this image bring words, other images or memories to mind? Do you feel a connection with something greater than yourself?

- As you continue in silent meditation, allow your soul to open and receive words, guidance, and love from the Divine. And,

- Stay with the image as long as you want.

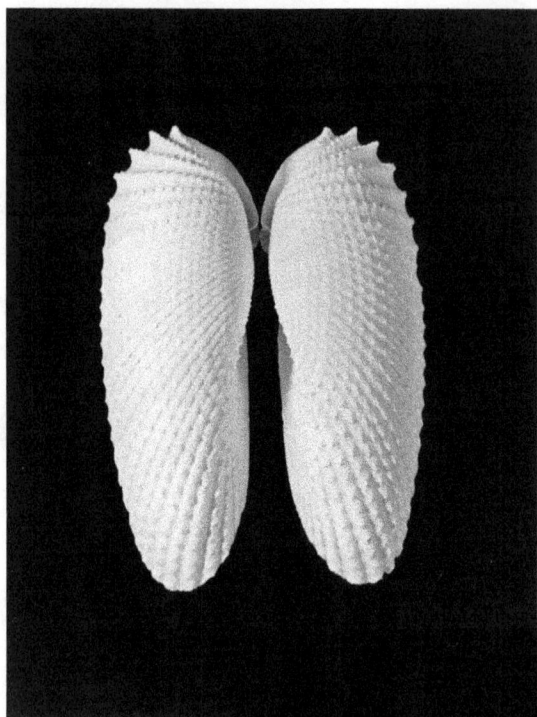

AT THE END
OF THE DAY OF REST

At the end of the day, life is too short to worry.

~ Lauren Ash

All good things must come to an end, and so it is with the Sabbath. But the closing of the special time need not be sad, as there will be another day of rest next week, and you can look forward to it already. Life's circular rhythm ensures that no daily or weekly ritual disappears for long.

Still, we need to mark the ending of Shabbat in some significant manner because it ushers in the return to the world of our regular, ordinary days.

The Jewish people have a beautiful closing ceremony called Havdalah (separation) during which it is customary to fill the ceremonial cup with wine all the way to the brim so that a little runs over the edge and spills when you pick it up. This symbolizes the wish for the coming week to overflow with an abundance of blessings.

The closing ritual also includes lighting a special braided candle which symbolizes the interconnectedness of all things and then extinguishing it in the remnants of wine from the shared cup. There are also fragrant spices and more blessings. You may choose to conclude with a prayer of gratitude for the fruits of the day of rest and a special blessing for the week to come.

Be mindful as you re-enter the ordinary world, and you can carry a reminder of the Sabbath with you.

REENTRY INTO THE REAL WORLD

That's the beauty of the Sabbath design;
it comes around weekly, so that,
when executed properly and consistently,
the practice spills over into regular time.

— J. Dana Trent

What do you do? What kind of rituals do you practice to get back into the swing of things? What discoveries during your day of rest can you bring into your regular life?

At our house, after the candle is extinguished, I start a load of laundry, water the plants, and record the time of next week's Sabbath in my notebook as well as on a chalkboard I keep in my kitchen. I review the list of items from my notebook and do any tasks that can be accomplished quickly and easily right away. Then I transfer any leftover items to the appropriate place: calendar, grocery list, to-do list. I review my calendar for the week and collect any items that I will need to accompany me on Monday morning when I leave for work.

You might want to lay out your clothes or put them on a hanger for the next day, and do the same for your children if they are young. Perhaps prepare lunch to take along ahead of time. The idea is to get a head start for Monday so that you can begin the week with a sense of calm and being organized.

Once you've established a Sabbath routine, occasionally ask yourself what you discovered about how it affected the rest of your week. How was that different from before? I believe you will find that your Sabbath routine and Sabbath heart have changed your life in ways both subtle and profound.

CONCLUSION

*The Sabbath command is an urgent summons
to break the pattern of the divided heart
...before it is too late.*

~ Walter Brueggemann

The Sabbath is an invitation to realign your days and your life. It has the power to set things right and provides both rest and freedom. We hope these writings and photographs have given you some inspiration and tools to begin your own way of keeping Sabbath. Now more than ever, we need rest and rhythms that will help create boundaries to make time for what matters most. Taking a day of rest allows us to discard our compulsions and helps us leave our worries at the threshold. The Sabbath offers us a timeout from frustrations, arguments, and resentments. It provides restorative rest. It is a pause that refreshes and brings with it all good things. We can relax and play, replenish ourselves and the world, and find nourishment for our weary bodies and souls.

Abraham Joshua Heschel, a 20th-century Jewish theologian, rabbi and philosopher, in his wonderful book, *The Sabbath*, describes what he calls "an architecture in time" and refers to the Sabbath as "our great cathedral." Providing a framework for transforming our lives, he states, "There is a realm of time where the goal is not to have but to be, not to own but to give, not to control but to share, not to subdue but to be in accord." Doesn't that sound like where we want to be? A day of rest can provide a framework for transforming our lives and create a space in which to truly live and move and have our being.

GENERAL GUIDELINES

- Start small.

- Remember that rest is the primary goal.

- Experiment with different ideas and see what fits into your life.

- Set boundaries on this time by lighting a candle or incense and reciting a prayer or poem, gazing at a piece of art or listening to music at the start.

- You might choose the same reading/piece of art/music each week or something new each time.

- Don't rush. Move leisurely.

- Steer clear of arguments or sadness.

- Make the Sabbath distinctly different from the other six days of the week.

- Keep Sabbath regular and consistent, preferably at the same time each week.

- Make it uniquely yours.

- Ponder what your Sabbath might look like:

  - What day and time will be your Sabbath?

  - Where will you be during this time?

  - What preparation do you need to take care of?

  - Guests to invite?

  - Groceries to buy?

  - What stressors do you want to keep at bay?

  - What is your intention?

  - How will you pay attention?

RESOURCES

BOOKS

Babb, Lynne M., *Sabbath: The Gift of Rest* and *Sabbath Keeping: Finding Freedoms in the Rhythms of Rest*

Berry, Wendell, *This Day: Sabbath Poems*

Brueggemann, Walter, *Sabbath as Resistance: Saying No to the Culture of Now*

Buchanan, Mark, T*he Rest of God: Restoring Your Soul by Restoring Sabbath*

Heschel, Abraham Joshua, *The Sabbath*

Miller, Shelly, *Rhythms of Rest*

Muller, Wayne, *Sabbath: Finding, Rest, Renewal, and Delight in our Busy Lives*

Phillips, Jan, *God is at Eye Level: Photography as a Healing Art*

Trent, J. Dana, *For Sabbath's Sake*

Sleeth, Matthew, *24/6 — A Prescription for a Healthier, Happier Life*

Shulevitz, Judith, *The Sabbath World*

Winner, Lauren F., *Mudhouse Sabbath*

RESOURCES FOR CHILDREN

Newman, Tracy, *Shabbat Is Coming*

Simpson, Leslie, *The Shabbat Box*

WEBSITES

chabad.org (for finding candle lighting times)

myjewishlearning.com

theshabbosproject.org

onetable.org

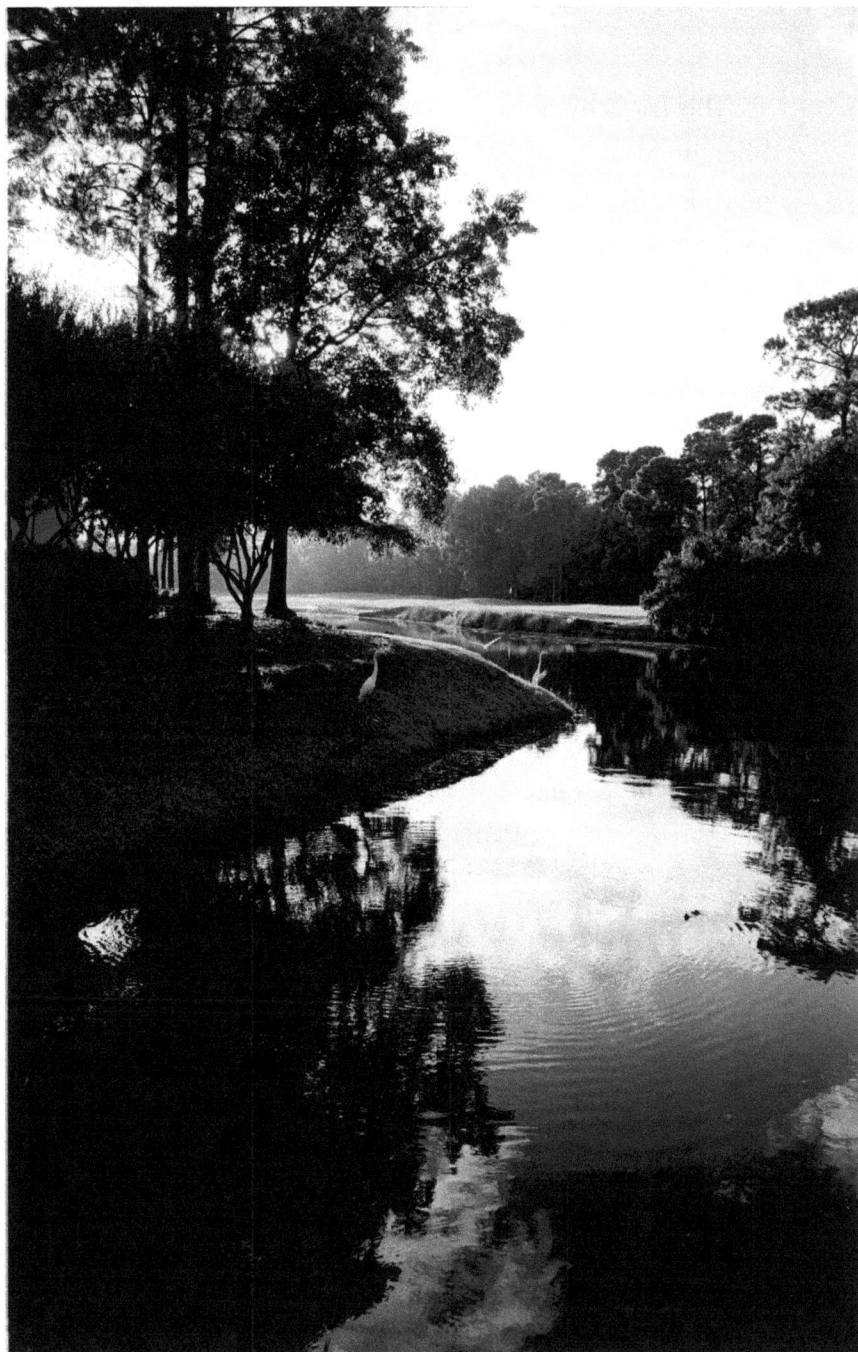

ADD/DELETE LIST

This list is by no means comprehensive since everyone has different ideas about what work and leisure activities might look like. Many items could easily belong to either column. Studying a topic of interest looks very different from studying for school. Cooking could go in either column depending on your approach. Others, like arguing or holding grudges, clearly belong in the delete column.

Go through the lists below and circle the ideas you'd like to add and cross out the ones to remove. Feel free to add your own ideas as well in the blank space included.

ADD	DELETE
Friends & family	Work
Solitary time	Technology
Contemplation	TV
Feasting	Computer
Study	Phone
Walking	Social Media
Meditation	Fasting
Being in Nature	Shopping
Forest Bathing	Spending money
Sleeping in	Errands
Napping	Chores
Fresh flowers	Arguing
Chocolates	Driving
Singing	Study
Music	Cooking

Games

Bird watching

Art

Writing

Worship

Gardening

Dressing up

Baking

Cooking

Gratitude

Blessings

Prayers

Playing

Day dreaming

Chanting

Yoga

Swimming

Cleaning

Exercise

Grudges

Clock watching

Sadness

Lawn mowing

Organized sports

Laundry

Schoolwork

Complaining

Criticism

Self doubt

_____

_____

_____

_____

_____

_____

LIST OF PHOTOGRAPHS

Cover Photo: Lake at Green Mountain Nature Trail,
Huntsville, AL

Page 3: The Indian Wall, built by Tom Hendrix

Page 6: The Van Dyke's porch

Page 9: Photography class with Maggie

Page 10: Limestone County tree

Page 13: 120-year-old dogwood tree at
Huntsville Botanical Gardens

Page 15: Ball canning jars and tangerine rind

Page 16: Seaside Florida beach

Page 21: Forest steps

Page 22: Boats on Clear Creek, Camp McDowell

Page 24: Lantern at the end of the day

Page 28: Aquatic Garden, Huntsville Botanical Garden

Page 31: Shells from Sanibel Island

Page 33: Katherine picks sunflowers

Page 34: Marsh on Hilton Head Island

Page 38: Nautilus shell

Page 40: Bicycles at Rosemary Beach

Page 42: Gate to the Bishop's Garden
at the National Cathedral, Washington, DC

Page 44: Sunset on the Gulf Coast

Page 46: Morning at Kanuga Conference Center

Page 47: Buddha snow globe

Page 49: Rowers at Ditto Landing on the Tennessee River

Page 50: White Tulips

Page 54-55: Ginkgo Tree, Fall and Winter

Page 57: Friends at Seaside Beach, FL

Page 60: Sabbath table

Page 62: Sabbath wine

Page 64: Challah made by Mushky Gerlitzke-Cohen

Page 67: Yellow Peppers

Page 68: Pears after the photographer gets hungry

ACKNOWLEDGMENTS

Marilyn

I'm deeply indebted to Chris Angermann for helping me to envision this dream. He contributed to this book in so many ways above and beyond his role as editor. I appreciate his constant encouragement and his ability to see the big picture.

I also very much appreciate Dan and Shellie Rubin, and Susan Angermann, for their willingness to read our manuscript and offer helpful suggestions and improvements.

I'll forever remember the late Shelly Miller who showed me how to enhance my practice and grow community.

Thanks to our Sabbath Circle participants: Ana, Catherine, Christine, Cindi, Cooper, Debbie, Dianna, Donna, Elizabeth, Freya, Jeff, and Nikki.

Thanks to the many people I met on my travels who shared their Sabbath experiences and stories with me.

And to my dear friend Nikki for sharing her beautiful images in the book and her steadfast collaboration on this journey.

I am grateful for my dear friends turned proof-readers: Cindi Branham, Donna Lamb, Lynette Lanphere, and Christine Starnes. I appreciate you eagle eyes and love of words more than you can ever know.

Finally, this book would never have happened without my sweet husband, Robin Cozby. I give thanks for his many gifts, his infinite patience, and his keen editor's eye. He is the best life traveling companion I could have dreamed up and has been a great sounding board.

ACKNOWLEDGMENTS

NIKKI

Thank you to my children, Michael, Eric, and Kelley Robbins, who give me the blessing of being called Mom; and to my grandchildren, Alexander and Maggie Robbins, who have blessed me to be Nana.

Thank you to my dear friend Marilyn, for the opportunity to be a part of this book.

Thanks to my marketing consultant, Nancy Hughes, who gave me a solid foundation for my photography journey.

And thank you for my Anam Cara, Susan Murphy.

I want to show my appreciation for my supportive group of Pachamamas—Beth Cook, Mary Catherine Akamatsu, Lynette Lanphere, Amy McBroom, Bernice Maze, and Jeanne Nelson—from whom I gathered spiritual strength during dark times in our lives. Thank you for our circle of energy.

My deep appreciation goes to Rabbi Moshe and Mushky Gerlitzky-Cohen, who opened their Sabbath table to teach me their customs, and to Pam Rhodes who enabled that journey.

Thanks to author/photographer Jan Phillips, who has given me inspiration through her photography books and teachings.

My gratitude also goes to many artists, too numerous to name, who have influenced the way that I see my world.

Finally, to Chris Angermann of Bardolf & Company: thank you for your masterful editing skills and your creative eye for the photographs.

MARILYN

Marilyn Lands grew up and lives in Huntsville, Alabama. As a Licensed Professional Counselor in the State of Alabama, she provides individual, family, and group counseling in a private practice setting. She is also licensed as a Supervising Counselor and works with clinicians to meet their requirements for State licensure.

Before entering private practice, Marilyn worked for over a decade in community mental health and is a passionate advocate for health issues. She has also worked in the banking and aerospace industries. Marilyn holds Master of Science degrees in Counseling Psychology and Management, and a Bachelor of Science degree in Business Administration.

She is a frequent lecturer and conducts specialized seminars on parenting, balanced living, stress management, Sabbath keeping, mindfulness meditation, and coping with grief. A member of the Episcopal Church of Nativity, she serves on the Commission for Spirituality in the diocese of Alabama.

NIKKI

Nikki Chenault was born in Tuscaloosa, grew up in Decatur, and attended the University of Alabama. She has worked in the defense industry, and built a successful stained-glass business, designing and executing commissioned glass artwork. As a photographer, she has taken specialized classes in nature photography and studied subjective lighting techniques for portraits. She now specializes in black and white photography, using only natural light.

Her works have been juried into art competitions throughout the southeastern United States, including the Seeing the Light Photography Exhibition at Washington, DC's National Cathedral, the Bi-state Art Association's Art Competition in Meridian, Mississippi, The Tennessee Valley Art Association's Art Competition in Tuscumbia, Alabama, and Unique Views of Huntsville, Huntsville Museum of Art. Her photos are available at *http://nikki-chenault. artistwebsites.com/index.html.*

Nikki is a member of St. Stephen's Episcopal Church. She has three grown children and two grandchildren.

We'd love to hear from you about your experience and approach to taking a day of rest, so please email us at:

marilynlands@gmail.com
and
nikkichenault@gmail.com

www.ingramcontent.com/pod-product-compliance
Lightning Source LLC
Chambersburg PA
CBHW072147090426
42739CB00013B/3310